UNDERSTANDING THE
HUMAN BODY

Digestion and Reproduction

by
Steve Parker

Please visit our web site at: www.garethstevens.com
For a free color catalog describing Gareth Stevens Publishing's list of high-quality
books and multimedia programs, call 1-800-542-2595 (USA) or 1-800-387-3178
(Canada). Gareth Stevens Publishing's fax: (414) 332-3567.

Library of Congress Cataloging-in-Publication Data

Parker, Steve.
    Digestion and reproduction / by Steve Parker.
        p. cm. — (Understanding the human body)
    Includes index.
    ISBN 0-8368-4205-7 (lib. bdg.)
    1. Digestive organs—Juvenile literature. 2. Generative organs—Juvenile literature. I. Title. II. Series.
QP145.P1644   2004
612.3—dc22   2004045329

This North American edition first published in 2005 by
Gareth Stevens Publishing
A World Almanac Education Group Company
330 West Olive Street, Suite 100
Milwaukee, WI 53212 USA

This U.S. edition copyright © 2005 by Gareth Stevens, Inc. Original edition copyright
© 2004 ticktock Entertainment Ltd. First published in Great Britain in 2004 by ticktock
Media Ltd., Unit 2, Orchard Business Centre, North Farm Road, Tunbridge Wells, Kent,
TN2 3XF.

We would like to thank Elizabeth Wiggans, Jenni Rainford, and Dr. Kristina Routh for
their help with this book.

Consultant: Dr. Kristina Routh
Gareth Stevens editor: Carol Ryback
Gareth Stevens designer: Scott M. Krall

Picture credits: t (top), b (bottom), c (center), l (left), r (right)
Alamy: Cover (left), 8–9c, 10tl, 10-11c, 11t, 11b, 29c, 29bc. Creatas: 12–13c. Primal
Pictures: 7tr, 13tr, 15tr, 15br, 16tl, 17tr, 17cr, 19tr, 21tr, 21cr. Science Photo Library:
4–5c, 7br, 13t, 14–15c, 16–17c, 17bc, 17br, 18–19c, 19br, 21br, 23tr, 23br, 26tl, 27b.
Wellcome Photo Library: 25r (all).

Printed in the United States of America

1 2 3 4 5 6 7 8 9 08 07 06 05 04

GARETH**STEVENS**
PUBLISHING
A World Almanac Education Group Company

How to use this book

This book is your guide to yourself—an atlas of the human body. Follow the main text for an informative overview of a particular area of the body or use the boxes to jump to a specific area of interest. Finally, try some of the suggested activities and experiments to discover more about yourself!

 Body Locator

Highlighted areas on the body locator help you learn your body's geography by indicating the area of the body organs or systems discussed on those pages.

 Instant Fact

Get instant, snappy facts that summarize the topic in just a few sentences. Learn where your internal organs are located, what they do, and how they work together.

👁 *Health Watch*

Read about illness and disease related to the relevant area of the body. For example, on the section about digestion, learn why eating certain foods can cause heartburn.

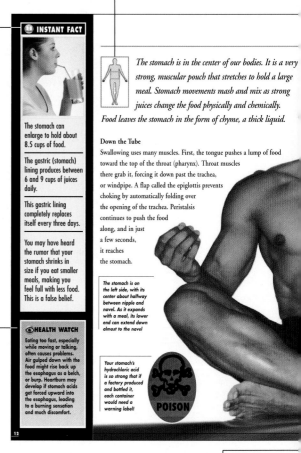

📖 INSTANT FACT

The stomach can enlarge to hold about 8.5 cups of food.

The gastric (stomach) lining produces between 6 and 9 cups of juices daily.

This gastric lining completely replaces itself every three days.

You may have heard the rumor that your stomach shrinks in size if you eat smaller meals, making you feel full with less food. This is a false belief.

👁 HEALTH WATCH

Eating too fast, especially while moving or talking, often causes problems. Air gulped down with the food might rise back up the esophagus as a belch, or burp. Heartburn may develop if stomach acids get forced upward into the esophagus, leading to a burning sensation and much discomfort.

12

The stomach is in the center of our bodies. It is a very strong, muscular pouch that stretches to hold a large meal. Stomach movements mash and mix as strong juices change the food physically and chemically. Food leaves the stomach in the form of chyme, a thick liquid.

Down the Tube
Swallowing uses many muscles. First, the tongue pushes a lump of food toward the top of the throat (pharynx). Throat muscles there grab it, forcing it down past the trachea, or windpipe. A flap called the epiglottis prevents choking by automatically folding over the opening of the trachea. Peristalsis continues to push the food along, and in just a few seconds, it reaches the stomach.

The stomach is on the left side, with its center about halfway between nipple and navel. As it expands with a meal, its lower end can extend down almost to the navel.

Your stomach's hydrochloric acid is so strong that if a factory produced and bottled it, each container would need a warning label!

POISON

🔬 *Diagrams*

Watch for in-depth scientific diagrams and explanations that focus on the details of a body part.

Metric Conversion Table on page 31

In Focus

View stunning macroimagery and other images of an anatomically correct digital model of body parts.

Squeeze, Squirm, Churn
The stomach does more than simply hold food before passing it to the next part of the digestive system. As the stomach fills, it squirms with forceful muscle contractions, squeezing and churning chewed food into a pulp. At the same time, about 35 million gastric glands in the stomach's lining release juices that attack the food inside with powerful hydrochloric acid, hormones, and enzymes. This "acid bath" not only breaks food down, but also helps kill most of the germs that came in on the food.

Radioactive barium shows up on X rays as pale or white areas. A barium meal fills the inside of the stomach, showing its shape and position, and reveals tumors and constrictions.

DIGESTION AND REPRODUCTION

IN FOCUS
SWALLOWING

tongue

muscles

trachea

The base of the tongue extends down into the neck and helps push food into the esophagus, which lies behind the trachea. Straplike muscles around the pharynx and larynx (voicebox) also help during swallowing.

TRY IT YOURSELF

Ask friends to point to where they think their stomach is. They may indicate their navel (belly button), but you know better! The stomach sits much higher, just beneath the ribs on your left side.

STOMACH AREAS
The stomach has three regions; gases collect in the fundus area. The stomach's three muscle-wall layers lie at different angles to each other. The duodenum is the first part of the small intestine.

duodenum — cardiac region
pyloric region — gastric body region
gastric fundus

Try It Yourself

Try these suggested activities to learn more. No special equipment is required—just your own body!

CONTENTS

Introduction

Your abdomen is the part of the body below the chest and above the legs. It contains the internal organs that produce special fluids that process your food into usable substances and into solid and liquid wastes. The abdomen also holds some of the male and most of the female reproductive organs.

Food and Drink

Digestion begins in the mouth. Your saliva (spit) contains watery chemicals that help soften food as the teeth mash it into smaller pieces. Liquids and chewed food are soon swallowed. Internal muscles slowly push food and drink down into the stomach, where it is broken down further by muscle contractions and a strong acid. From there, it passes into the small intestine—where most of the absorption of nutrients occurs—and then into the large intestine.

Waste Disposal (Excretory System)

Unusable, excess solid material empties out of the lower end of the large intestine at the base of the abdomen. The urinary system—which has no direct connection with the digestive system—produces and removes liquid waste, or urine. This straw-colored liquid consists of by-products and excess water filtered from the bloodstream. A stretchy baglike organ, the bladder, stores the urine until it is convenient for you to release it.

Long-Term Survival

The reproductive system is not essential for survival of an individual. But it is vital for the long-term survival of the human species. The "product" of the reproductive system eats and drinks, eliminates waste, cries, sleeps, and is a helpless bundle—a baby.

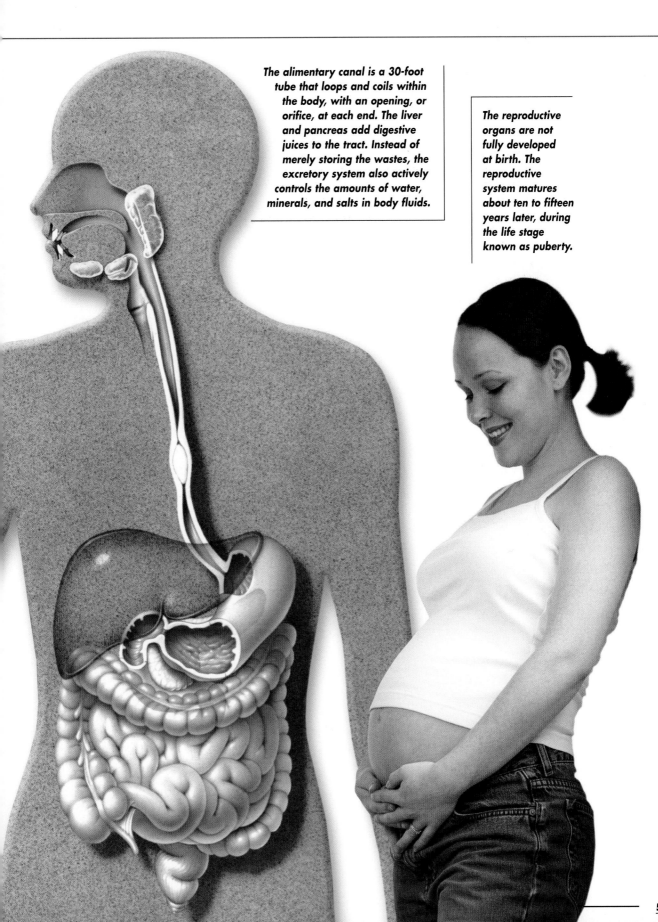

The alimentary canal is a 30-foot tube that loops and coils within the body, with an opening, or orifice, at each end. The liver and pancreas add digestive juices to the tract. Instead of merely storing the wastes, the excretory system also actively controls the amounts of water, minerals, and salts in body fluids.

The reproductive organs are not fully developed at birth. The reproductive system matures about ten to fifteen years later, during the life stage known as puberty.

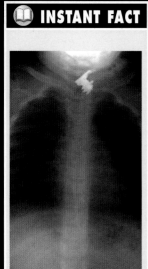
Digestion *Digestive System*

After savoring the delicious flavors of a well-chewed mouthful of food, you swallow it, seemingly putting an end to the matter. But the food has only begun its lengthy and complicated digestive journey. It now moves through the body at an average speed of about one foot per hour.

Our bodies use energy from food and liquids to think, breathe, move, and even digest our meals.

The outer curve of the stomach measures about twelve inches.

Food takes between 15 and 48 hours to move through the entire 30 feet of the digestive tract, or alimentary canal.

Gulp!

The digestive system has about a dozen major parts that come into action one after the other. Food's first encounter with the body is the mouth. Here the teeth slice and crush it, the tongue tastes it and moves it around for thorough chewing, and watery saliva from the salivary glands moistens the food. As you swallow, food enters the soft tube called the esophagus that leads through the chest to the stomach.

Stomach and Intestines

After a few hours of physical and chemical "attack" in the stomach, the mashed, liquidy "chyme" passes into the small intestine—a narrow and very long tube that twists and coils to fit inside the abdomen. The small intestine continues the digestive process by absorbing into the bloodstream nutrients from what was once a meal of chicken or pizza, or a snack such as carrots or ice cream.

Any food waste left over passes into the large intestine, where water is taken from it according to the body's needs. Finally, the wastes are compacted and stored in the rectum before exiting the body through the anus.

Organs That Aid Digestion

Two internal organs, the pancreas and liver, also play vital roles in digestion. The pancreas produces powerful juices that flow into the small intestine to aid chemical digestion. The liver receives most of the digested nutrients from the small intestine.

Food production is an enormous, worldwide industry. It requires a lot of land, water, and energy to grow, harvest, process, pack, transport, and sell the meats, vegetables, grains, and fruits that go into our digestive systems.

As compost—leftover foods, garden wastes, and similar materials—rots in a biodigester, it releases a burnable gas called methane. The body's digestive system also releases burnable gases as it digests food.

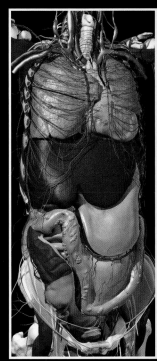

The abdomen, the largest body cavity, is hardly an empty space. The folded digestive tract is packed into the abdomen below the liver and stomach.

"We are what we eat" is perfectly true. Our bodies keep us alive and growing by using substances found in our food.

🖐 TRY IT YOURSELF

Slow down during your next meal. Sit quietly before and after eating. Chew each mouthful ten to twenty times. Savor the flavors and enjoy the food's textures, separately and combined.

🐌 PERISTALSIS AND DIGESTION

Food doesn't just fall through the body from our mouth on down. It is pushed or massaged along the digestive tract by peristalsis— wavelike muscle contractions of the tract's walls. Digestive processes are carefully timed so that, as food moves on its journey, different areas of the tract

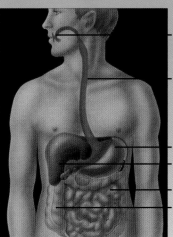

- mouth
- esophagus
- stomach
- liver
- small intestine
- large intestine

become active one after the other. The brain sends nerve signals that release the "messenger" chemicals, or hormones, into the bloodstream and control peristalsis and the digesitve process.

The average person eats about half a ton of food each year.

A calorie measures the amount of energy contained in that food. Food labels list calorie content per serving.

Different foods provide the following amounts of calories per gram:
carbohydrates 4
proteins 4
fats 9

A 130-pound person burns about this many calories per minute:
reading 1.5
walking 3.1
jogging 5.7

Digestion *Nutritional Needs*

The body requires a range of different foods for good health. It needs a steady supply of moderate amounts of the three main food groups— proteins, carbohydrates, and fats—and their fiber, vitamins, and minerals for a balanced diet.

Carbohydrates

We get most of our energy from carbohydrates. They are broken down into various sugars, especially glucose. Potatoes, wheat, rice, oats, barley, refined sugars, and various fruits and vegetables all contain carbohydrates.

Proteins

We get protein from meats, fish, eggs, other dairy products, and some vegetables— especially peas and beans. Proteins are the body's main building materials that help babies and children grow into adults. Our bodies also use proteins to maintain and repair body organs such as muscles.

Fats and Oils

Our nerves use energy from the fats and oils we eat. Animal sources of fat and oils include meat, butter, and lard, which contain saturated fats and cholesterol and may contribute to heart disease. Vegetables, fruits, nuts, and seeds, such as corn, cashews, and pumpkin seeds, may also contain some fats and oils— but do not contain cholesterol.

Vitamins and Minerals

Our bodies need the small but regular amounts of vitamins and minerals found in most foods—especially fresh fruits and vegetables. Vitamin K in spinach helps our blood clot, while Vitamin C in strawberries helps us fight illnesses. Meat contains the mineral iron, which helps red blood cells carry oxygen throughout the body, while calcium in milk and cheese makes teeth and bones strong.

Fiber

Many plant foods contain fiber. Although it is not absorbed by the body, fiber helps move food through the intestines, reducing the risk of digestive problems. Rice, corn, oatmeal, fresh fruits, leafy vegetable, beans, and lentils are all rich in fiber.

Many people in the industrialized countries are overweight. Health experts consider obesity an epidemic because it affects large numbers of people and raises their health risks.

Some animals, such as mosquitoes, vampire bats, leeches, and fleas, thrive by eating a very simple, nutritious diet—blood. Our bodies are designed for a much wider range and variety of foods.

IN FOCUS
ENERGY VS. NUTRIENTS

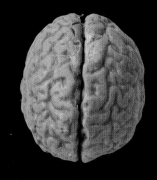

The brain uses far more energy for its size than any other body organ. It consumes one-fifth of all the energy in food, even though it makes up just one-fiftieth of the body's total weight.

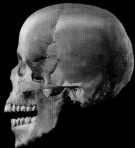

In contrast, bones use just one-hundredth of the energy, weight for weight, compared to the brain. Bones require a far greater proportion of minerals, especially calcium, phosphate, and sulfate, than any other body organ.

TRY IT YOURSELF

Read some of the nutrition labels on food to see how many calories they contain. Which foods do you think are the healthiest for you?

FOOD VARIETY

This color-coded pie chart displays some foods that contribute to a balanced diet (starting from top left): bread, cereal, and grains; fresh fruit and vegetables; cheese and milk; sugar and starches; fish, meat, and eggs. (Beans and peas are also packed with protein.)

Your jaw grows as you do, so you needed two sets of teeth—"baby" (deciduous) teeth and permanent teeth. These poke through the gums at the following ages:

Front teeth (incisors)
6–12 months

Lateral (side) incisors
9–15 months

Canines ("eyeteeth")
15–24 months

Bicuspids (premolars)
15–20 months

Tricuspids (molars)
24–30 months

Your adult set of thirty-two teeth emerges after about six or seven years.

Digestion *Mouth and Teeth*

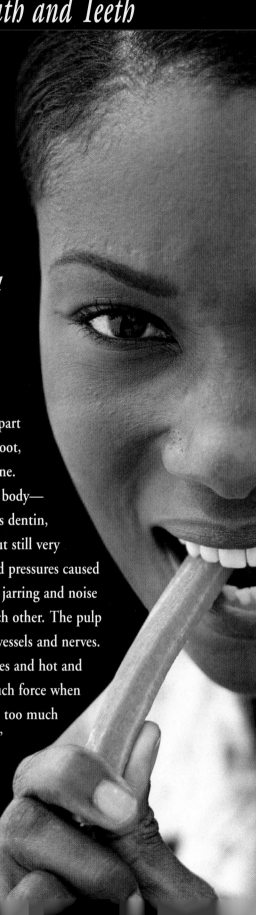

Look in a mirror, smile, and stick out your tongue to view your first line of digestive "weapons." As teeth cut and crush food, the tongue moves it around to make sure every piece is thoroughly chewed.

The Structure of Teeth

Each tooth consists of the crown, the part that shows outside the gums, and its root, which is firmly anchored in the jawbone. Enamel—the hardest substance in the body— covers a tooth's crown. Underneath lies dentin, which is slightly softer than enamel but still very tough. Dentin helps absorb shocks and pressures caused by biting and chewing and lessens the jarring and noise produced when teeth meet food or each other. The pulp inside the dentin contains tiny blood vessels and nerves. These sensitive nerves detect toothaches and hot and cold temperatures and warn of too much force when biting. (Teeth can snap or crack under too much pressure.) A layer of cementum "glues" tooth roots into the jawbone.

Scientists constantly develop and test new flavors in hopes of producing food that stimulates your tongue's ten thousand taste buds.

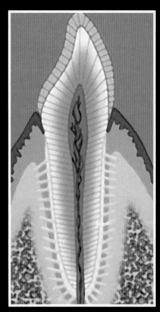

Your teeth will last a lifetime if you take care of them by brushing, flossing, and visiting the dentist regularly.

The Tongue and Salivary Glands

Your tongue is a band of muscles that bends more than any other muscle in the body. It pushes food around the mouth, holds it for crushing by the teeth, and helps you swallow. Your three pairs of salivary glands—located below the ears, in the angle of the jaw, and under the tongue—produce more than six cups of watery saliva every day. Saliva helps your taste buds work. It also contains chemicals that begin the digestive process, and it lubricates food so you can swallow it.

A cutaway canine tooth shows its tall pointed shape, outer enamel with dentin underneath, and delicate dental pulp. The root is twice as long as its crown to help stabilize the tooth from pressures when we bite and tear at food.

The long, sharp edges of the front teeth are designed for biting and cuting off chunks from large pieces of food.

TONSILS

Germs, along with food and air, enter the body through the mouth. Lumpy masses, called tonsils, on each side of the throat catch germs. A sore throat and painful tonsilitis occur when too many germs overwhelm and swell the tonsil tissues.

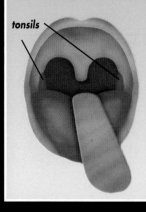

tonsils

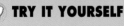 TRY IT YOURSELF

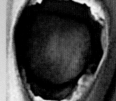

Look in a mirror and open wide to see the different shapes of your upper and lower teeth. The eight front incisors have sharp edges for biting. Next come four taller, pointy canines, or "eyeteeth," for tearing. Eight bicuspids and twelve tricuspids (including the four wisdom teeth) mash and grind your food. Teeth can have one, two, or three roots.

The stomach can enlarge to hold about 8.5 cups of food.

The gastric (stomach) lining produces between 6 and 9 cups of juices daily.

This gastric lining completely replaces itself every three days.

You may have heard the rumor that your stomach shrinks in size if you eat smaller meals, making you feel full with less food. This is a false belief.

◉ HEALTH WATCH

Eating too fast, especially while moving or talking, often causes problems. Air gulped down with the food might rise back up the esophagus as a belch, or burp. Heartburn may develop if stomach acids get forced upward into the esophagus, leading to a burning sensation and much discomfort.

Digestion *Stomach*

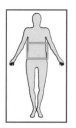

The stomach is in the center of our bodies. It is a very strong, muscular pouch that stretches to hold a large meal. Stomach movements mash and mix as strong juices change the food physically and chemically. Food leaves the stomach in the form of chyme, a thick liquid.

Down the Tube

Swallowing uses many muscles. First, the tongue pushes a lump of food toward the top of the throat (pharynx). Throat muscles there grab it, forcing it down past the trachea, or windpipe. A flap called the epiglottis prevents choking by automatically folding over the opening of the trachea. Peristalsis continues to push the food along, and in just a few seconds, it reaches the stomach.

The stomach is on the left side, with its center about halfway between nipple and navel. As it expands with a meal, its lower end can extend down almost to the navel

Your stomach's hydrochloric acid is so strong that if a factory produced and bottled it, each container would need a warning label!

POISON

IN FOCUS
SWALLOWING

Squeeze, Squirm, Churn

The stomach does more than simply hold food before passing it to the next part of the digestive system. As the stomach fills, it squirms with forceful muscle contractions, squeezing and churning chewed food into a pulp. At the same time, about 35 million gastric glands in the stomach's lining release juices that attack the food inside with powerful hydrochloric acid, hormones, and enzymes. This "acid bath" not only breaks food down, but also helps kill most of the germs that came in on the food.

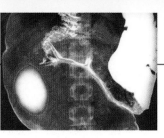

Radioactive barium shows up on X rays as pale or white areas. A barium meal fills the inside of the stomach, showing its shape and position, and reveals tumors and constrictions.

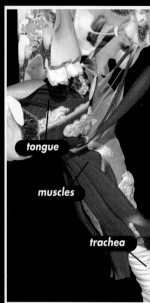

tongue

muscles

trachea

The base of the tongue extends down into the neck and helps push food into the esophagus, which lies behind the trachea. Straplike muscles around the pharynx and larynx (voicebox) also help during swallowing.

TRY IT YOURSELF

Ask friends to point to where they think their stomach is. They may indicate their navel (belly button), but you know better! The stomach sits much higher, just beneath the ribs on your left side.

STOMACH AREAS

The stomach has four regions; gases collect in the fundus area. The stomach's three muscle-wall layers lie at different angles to each other. The duodenum is the first part of the small intestine.

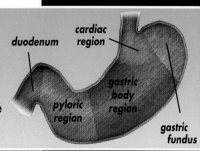

duodenum

cardiac region

gastric body region

pyloric region

gastric fundus

Digestion *Intestines*

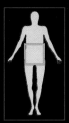

We often say "guts" when referring to our stomachs and intestines (bowels). Oddly, our small intestines take up much more space inside our bodies than our large intestines.

Nutrient Absorption Area

If you could straighten out your small intestine, it would stretch to about seven times your height. Thousands of tiny fingerlike projections—"villi"—each about one millimeter tall and covered in "microvilli," line the inside of the small intestine and act like a towel to soak up liquids. These factors provide an enormous surface area that allows for the absorption of most of the nutrients in your food. The intestinal lining also secretes enzymes and other chemicals that finish digesting the chyme (pulped food)— which passes from the stomach into the small intestine in small, regular "squirts" through a muscular ring called the pyloric sphincter. Minute blood and lymph vessels within the villi absorb nutrients into your bloodstream.

The small intestine produces six to nine cups of digestive juices each day.

Foods pass through the small intestine for up to six hours.

Your intestinal lining has a total surface area that is almost twice as large as the skin area of your entire body..

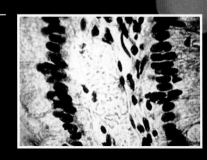

stomach

small intestine

large intestine (colon)

Each villus contains a network of tiny blood vessels, called venules and arterioles, as well as a central canal that contains a lymph vessel. These vessels soak up nutrients from digested food and carry them around the body.

Eating too fast or not chewing food properly may cause stomach cramps. Germs from tainted food, an infection, or a blockage can also cause internal pain. X rays and other diagnostic tests help doctors identify serious intestinal problems.

IN FOCUS
INSIDE THE ABDOMEN

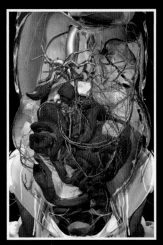

A cutaway view (without the stomach, liver, and large intestine) shows the small intestine coiled around the lower half of the abdomen.

Nearing the End

The small intestine connects to the large intestine. At the junction of the two hangs a hollow, finger-sized "dead end"—the appendix. Tiny pieces of food and germs sometimes get caught in it and cause appendicitis. The main job of the large intestine, which is twice as wide as the small intestine and about the same length as your body's height, is to remove excess water and minerals from the remaining food. The rectum stores any leftover products as unpleasant brown lumps, or "feces," until they pass through the anus.

The colon (large intestine) forms a "frame" around the small bowel.

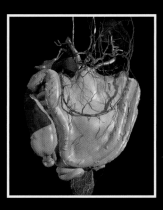

A curtain of fat called the omentum drapes over the front of the lower abdomen to cushion and protect the internal organs.

anus

🔬 INTESTINAL VILLI

Intestinal villi form an irregular inner surface lining that resembles the pile of terry cloth or carpeting. Muscle layers within the small intestine's wall squirm and squeeze digested food along.

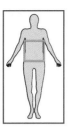

The liver is the body's largest internal organ. It weighs between three and four pounds.

The liver produces one quart of bile daily. Bile breaks down fat globules by changing their surface tension, which helps digestive enzymes work better.

The liver contains more blood, in proportion to its size, than almost any other organ.

Jaundice is a sympton of liver trouble that turns the skin and eyes yellow. A healthy liver breaks down old red blood cells and removes their coloring substance (pigment). This gives bile, a liver fluid that is normally released into the intestines, its color. In a diseased liver, the bile pigment instead builds up in body tissues, changing the normal coloring of a person. Hepatitis is a viral or bacterial infection of the liver that causes jaundice.

Digestion *Liver and Pancreas*

Only the brain "multitasks" better than the liver. Most of the more than five hundred different biological functions performed by the liver involve regulating the body chemistry.

Your Busy Liver

Your liver receives blood from two sources. Oxygen-rich blood flows directly from the heart, while nutrient-rich blood flows up from the intestines. The liver uses nutrients according to the body's needs. When it detects high blood sugar levels, the liver changes some of that blood sugar (glucose) into its storable form—glycogen. As blood sugar runs low, the liver converts some of that glycogen back into glucose. The liver also stores and releases many other substances, such as blood and vitamins.

The liver detoxifies—makes harmless—poisons (toxins) such as alcohol and other drugs. An overworked liver becomes fibrous and hard, leading to a serious disease called cirrhosis of the liver.

liver

Detoxification—the breaking down and neutralizing of toxins—is one of the liver's most important tasks. The liver also produces bile, a liquid that is stored in the gallbladder (a small bag beneath the liver). After a meal, bile flows from the gallbladder through the bile duct into the small intestine, where it helps digest fatty foods.

Two Jobs

In contrast to the liver, the pancreas performs only two main functions. It produces digestive enzymes that ooze along the pancreatic duct into the small intestine after a meal. The pancreas also secretes the hormones glucagon and insulin directly into the bloodstream.

stomach

The lower right ribs partially protect the right side of the wedge-shaped liver as it extends from about nipple level almost down to the waist. The pancreas lies across the body just behind and below the stomach and rests in the curve of the small intestine.

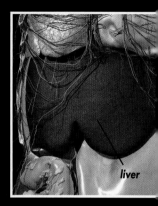

liver

The liver is pressed against the base of the chest under the diaphragm, with most of its bulk on the right side. It gets its dark red color from its massive blood content.

pancreas

The soft, six-inch-long, gray-pink pancreas is the body's second-largest gland, after the liver. It lies crossways in the abdomen.

👆 TRY IT YOURSELF

Have you ever noticed how a young child's tummy appears overly large? The liver, not the stomach, causes the bulging belly. Compared to an adult, a baby's liver is much larger in proportion to the rest of its body. The liver takes up almost half of a baby's entire abdomen but only one-quarter of an adult's abdomen.

🔬 INSIDE THE PANCREAS AND LIVER

liver lobule

liver

gall bladder

pancreas

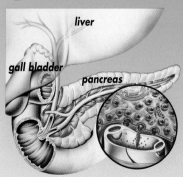

Tiny bunches of cells within the pancreas (left) make digestive juices. Some pancreatic cells also produce hormones. The liver (right) contains thousands of six-sided units called lobules, each about one millimeter across. Every liver lobule has its own blood vessels and tubes for the bile (shown in green) that flows to the gallbladder

Digestion *Getting Rid of Wastes*

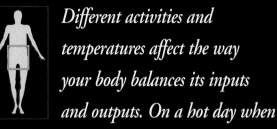

Different activities and temperatures affect the way your body balances its inputs and outputs. On a hot day when rushing around, you may drink a lot but not need a restroom for hours. On a cold day with little movement, you may need to visit a restroom more frequently.

Removing the Wastes

The body produces gaseous, solid, and liquid wastes. A waste gas called carbon dioxide leaves the lungs with each breath. Waste solids (feces) leave once or twice daily, while liquid waste (urine) leaves many times. Your kidneys—two compact organs that sit on either side of your spine in the upper abdomen—enjoy a very plentiful blood supply. Inside each kidney, about one million microfilters (nephrons) remove unwanted substances and extra water from the blood and produce urine. Some of these nephrons remain idle, which gives the kidneys enormous reserve capacity.

kidney

Many animals mark their territories by urinating and leaving piles of dung.

IN FOCUS
KIDNEYS AND BLADDER

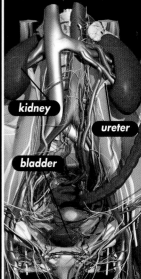

Massive renal arteries (red) and veins (blue) indicate the kidneys' huge blood supply. A pale-colored ureter from each kidney drains urine into the bladder.

Your kidneys ride high against the back wall of the abdomen, shielded by fat and the lower ribs. The left kidney sits slightly higher than the right. The bladder is in the front base of the abdomen.
This diagram shows the kidneys nearer to the front of the body to give you a better idea of their location.

ureter

kidney

ladder

ethra

Drip, Drip, Drip

The approximately 1 to 2 quarts of urine made daily collect in the central area, the renal pelvis, of each kidney. Urine flows down two 10-inch tubes—called ureters—that connect each kidney to the bladder. As the bladder gradually fills and stretches with urine, its owner feels the urge to urinate, or empty the bladder. Two sphincter muscles control the release of urine. As the bladder's internal urethral sphincter relaxes, urine flows down into the urethra. When we release the external urethral sphincter, the urine leaves our bodies. Urine production varies according to intake and activity levels.

TRY IT YOURSELF

Keep track of how much fluid you drink and how often you visit a restroom on days with very different temperature ranges. On hot days, you sweat more and produce less urine. On cooler days, you still sweat, but you may never notice it. Meanwhile, you may urinate often.

RENAL NEPHRONS

A glomerulus, the ball-shaped knot of capillary blood vessels that serves as the workhorse of each renal nephron, is surrounded by a double-walled Bowman's capsule—from which extends a tubule called a loop of Henle. Wastes, minerals, and water pass from the blood into the tubule. Useful substances return to the blood, leaving urine.

nephron   glomerulus   capsule

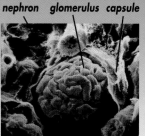

Digestion *Chemical Control*

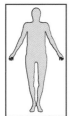

In addition to nerve action, your brain also controls the production and secretion of special chemicals, called hormones, directly into your bloodstream. These hormones, and the tissues and glands that produce them, comprise the endocrine system.

Two Systems

Your brain controls the body's electrical and chemical control systems. Like biological electricity, nerve signals zip around the body instantly to control muscles, heartbeat, breathing, and many other rapid-action processes. The chemical control system, the endocrine system, takes longer to react, but its effects linger. Your endocrine glands produce and release natural chemicals, called hormones, that travel through the body in the blood to affect certain organs, usually by making them work faster or slower.

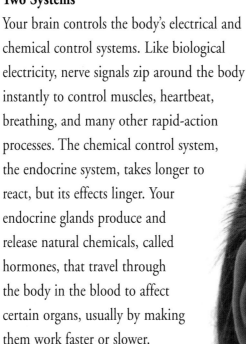

Corticoid hormones from the outer part (cortex) of the adrenal glands help the body cope with long-term stress. Adrenaline from the inner layer (medulla) readies us instantly for quick action—for example, to escape sudden danger.

Diabetes is a serious disease that occurs when the pancreas makes incorrect amounts of the hormone insulin. Many diabetics—people with diabetes—must inject insulin into their bodies every day of their lives.

IN FOCUS
HORMONAL GLANDS

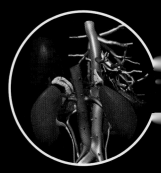

Adrenal glands—the pale curved triangles above—are also called the suprarenal glands because they ride atop each kidney.

Small but Important

Our bodies produce more than 100 hormones. The pea-sized pituitary gland that hangs just under the front of the brain produces about ten hormones, including a growth hormone that regulates the body's long-term development. It also secretes several hormones that control the production of other hormones, such as those made by the pancreas, ovaries, and testes.

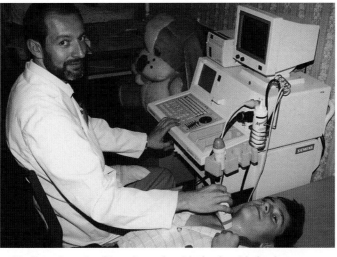

This doctor is testing his patient's thyroid. The thyroid gland stores and uses iodine to produce important hormones, including thyroxin (T_4). Thyroid hormones help regulate nearly all body processes.

The thyroid gland wraps around the front of the trachea just below the larynx. Its wide left and right lobes join at a narrow middle section, giving it an almost "butterfly" shape.

TRY IT YOURSELF

Next time someone surprises you, check your pulse. The hormone adrenaline has probably caused a faster heartbeat and increased blood flow to your muscles, making them ready for action.
This is known as the "fight or flight" response.

SEX HORMONES

During puberty, males and females begin producing increased amounts of sex hormones that cause major body changes. In males, the testes dramatically increase their production of testosterone, the main male sex hormone. In females, the ovaries begin producing more estrogen and progesterone.

Each ovary is about half an inch wide and an inch long—smaller than your thumb.

From a total of 200,000 in each ovary, a woman releases between 400 and 500 eggs in her lifetime.

Each testicle measures about two inches by one inch. A man produces many thousands of sperm cells every second, for a total of roughly 200 million every single day.

HEALTH WATCH

An unhealthy diet, lack of sleep, stress, and drugs such as alcohol can affect egg or sperm production. If a woman's eggs do not ripen or a man's sperm count is too low, that couple may not be able to produce a baby. This condition is known as infertility. Sometimes, simple treatments can solve the problem. In other cases, a more serious problem that may require advanced medical procedures exists.

Reproduction *Babies*

Waaaaaah! Caring for a totally helpless baby is often very noisy—and tiring. But having babies (reproduction) is essential to the continuation of our species. The type of reproductive organs determine whether a person is female or male.

The Menstrual Cycle

The female reproductive organs, the ovaries, are located on either side of the lower abdomen. About once a month after the female reaches sexual maturity, one of the ovaries releases a "ripe" egg cell. Over several days, this egg drifts down the fallopian tube toward the uterus. If no male reproductive cells (sperm) are present, the egg—along with the blood-rich uterine lining—passes out of the body through the vagina (birth canal), as the "period," or menstrual flow. Hormones cause this menstrual cycle to begin all over again.

From birth, every single human is a unique combination of separate traits for personality, wishes, and wants. Even identical twins, who are genetically identical "clones," develop different personalities.

IN FOCUS
OVARIES & SPERM

In the ovary, an egg ripens within a small fluid bag, or follicle. Ovulation occurs at midpoint of this cycle when the follicle ruptures (breaks open) and the egg enters the fallopian tube (oviduct).

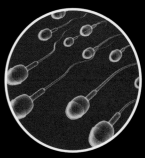

In the testes, sperm begin as blob-shaped spermatocytes around the inner edge of each seminiferous tubule. After about ten weeks, they "ripen" into mature sperm with tails that propel them on their journey to the outside of the body.

> Reproduction is a basic process of all plants and animals. In humans, it also involves complicated feelings of affection, friendship, love, and desire.

Sperm Production

Inside each testicle, or testis, a constant supply of tadpole-shaped sperm forms around the clock in long coiled tubes known as seminiferous tubules. The testes remain cooler than body temperature by their placement below the front abdomen within a skin pouch, the scrotum. A long tube, the epididymis, next to each testis stores sperm. During sex, fluids containing sperm travel down the vas deferens tube through the prostate gland to yet another tube, the urethra, and out through the penis.

🖌 REPRODUCTIVE SYSTEMS

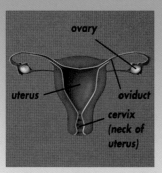

ovary

uterus

oviduct

cervix (neck of uterus)

Straplike ligaments hold the ovaries in position slightly above and behind the uterus ("womb") in the lower abdomen. The fallopian tubes, also called oviducts, lead to the pear-shaped uterus. The ovaries alternately release an egg a month.

The testes' position outside the abdomen keeps them slightly cooler than the main body. Temperature affects sperm production—fewer sperm form when the testes become too warm. A lower sperm count may affect the male's ability to reproduce.

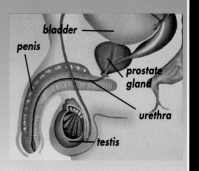

bladder

penis

prostate gland

urethra

testis

Three weeks after fertilization, the tiny heart is pulsing. Total body length is 2.5 mm.

After four weeks, the total body length has doubled. Limb buds for arms and legs appear.

At five weeks, the brain enlarges, the heart has four chambers, and the internal organs grow. Length is 8 mm.

After six weeks, the embryo still has a tail, its face begins forming, limbs lengthen, and hands and feet appear. Length is about half an inch (13 mm).

HEALTH WATCH

A mother's health is very important to her growing child. Smoking, drinking alcohol, and taking certain drugs, even for medical reasons, may harm the fetus. Too little food and a lack of nutrients may harm a fetus's development. Diseases, such as rubella (German measles), may also interfere with organ formation or proper fetal growth during pregnancy.

Reproduction *The Body Begins*

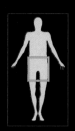

Each of the more than six billion people in the world began in exactly the same way: a tiny egg cell united with an even tinier sperm cell. This process occurs everywhere around the world (more than three times each second), and nine months later, many babies are born.

Fertilization

As a ripe egg cell (ovum) drifts slowly along one of the fallopian tubes, it may suddenly meet thousands of sperm cells "swimming" toward it. The sperm travel a long way from inside the man's body into the woman's body and through her uterus. Fertilization occurs when one of the sperm cells penetrates the egg. At that moment, the genetic material from mother and father combine. This fertilized egg cell continues to drift along the fallopian tube toward the uterus. Within days, it begins dividing to form a hollow, fluid-filled ball, or blastocyst, that may eventually implant itself into the uterine wall lining and begin its next growth phase as an embryo.

IN FOCUS
EMBRYO GROWTH

Immediately after fertilization, a human egg shows no signs of developing into an embryo.

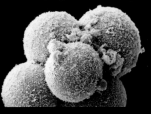

After 2–3 days, the embryo's cells start to divide.

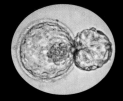

After about a week, the embryo implants itself in the wall of the uterus.

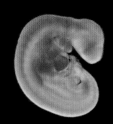

After implantation, the embryo continues to grow and takes on a more recognizable form. The embryo pictured above is about four weeks old.

In the Uterus

About a week after fertilization, the tiny embryo (as big as the dot on this "i") settles into the lining of the uterus, which contains a rich supply of blood and nutrients as part of the menstrual cycle. Cells of the embryo continue to divide and change shape as they specialize into different types of cells that form various tissues and organs. Eight weeks after fertilization, the grape-sized embryo resembles a miniature human body. By now, all of its main body parts are formed and ready for further growth.

A seven-week-old embryo floats in a bag filled with amniotic fluid. The yolk sac that provided nourishment during earlier stages has shrunk to a tiny "balloon" (red sac at left).

SPERM MEETS EGG

A sperm is tiny compared to the egg. Its rounded head end contains genetic material from the father. Fertilization occurs when one sperm finally burrows through the outer layer of an egg.

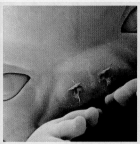
After four months, the fetus's bones begin to harden, and tiny buds that will become teeth form under the gums. Girls can be told apart from boys.

After six months, the stomach and intestines are fully formed, the nostrils open, and the fetus may suck its thumb.

After eight months, fat collects under the skin as overall growth starts slowing down. Chances of survival are good for a baby born during this development stage.

HEALTH WATCH

Prenatal (before birth) checkups monitor the general health of the mother and fetus and are very important during pregnancy. Some problems with pregnancy do not appear until they become serious and may not develop for many months. Proper prenatal care helps ensure a healthy birth and allows for early treatment of any problems.

Reproduction *Birth*

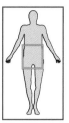

From three months after fertilization until birth, the developing baby is called a fetus. Most of this time is spent growing larger and adding finishing touches and details, such as hair and nails, to the body.

Inside the Uterus

For the first seven months of growth, a fetus increases its length and size by more than ten times. It floats in protective amniotic fluid as it grows. At first, the fetus can wave its arms, kick its legs, and do somersaults. Later, as the fetus grows larger, it becomes cramped and moves less. In the middle of pregnancy, the fetus is slim and wrinkled. Near the end, a layer of fat collects under the skin so the newborn appears chubby.

Birth Day

After nine months, birth is near. Strong contractions of the muscular uterine walls gradually push the baby out through the cervix (neck of the uterus), through the vagina, (birth canal), and out into the world. Birth may be quick or take many hours. It is a very tiring ordeal for both mother and baby.

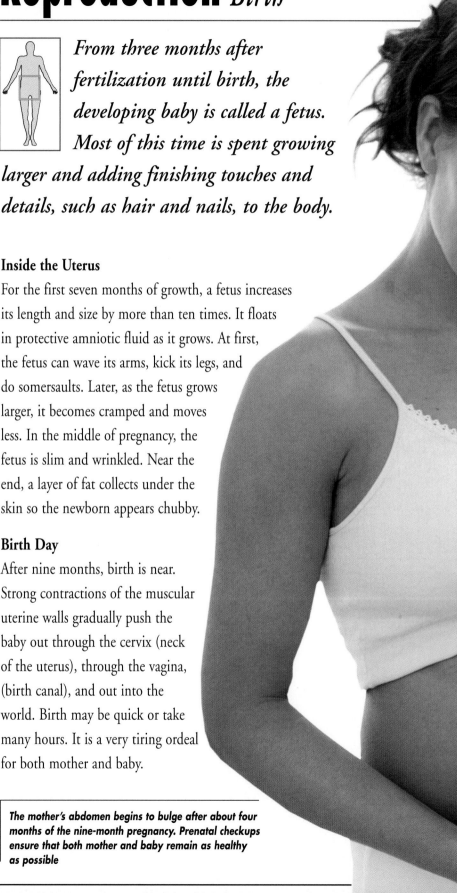

The mother's abdomen begins to bulge after about four months of the nine-month pregnancy. Prenatal checkups ensure that both mother and baby remain as healthy as possible

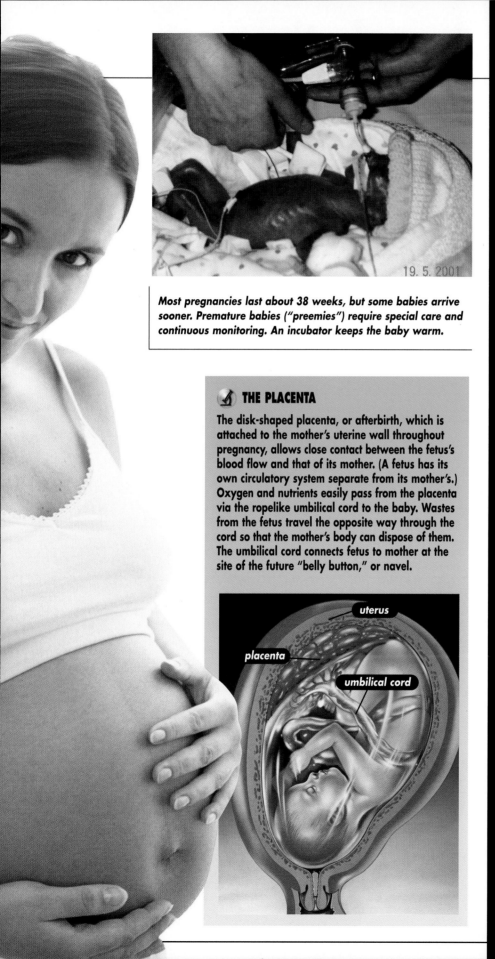

IN FOCUS
GROWING FETUS

After just a few weeks, the embryo slowly takes on a more human appearance, with hands, feet, and head recognizable.

Most pregnancies last about 38 weeks, but some babies arrive sooner. Premature babies ("preemies") require special care and continuous monitoring. An incubator keeps the baby warm.

🔖 THE PLACENTA

The disk-shaped placenta, or afterbirth, which is attached to the mother's uterine wall throughout pregnancy, allows close contact between the fetus's blood flow and that of its mother. (A fetus has its own circulatory system separate from its mother's.) Oxygen and nutrients easily pass from the placenta via the ropelike umbilical cord to the baby. Wastes from the fetus travel the opposite way through the cord so that the mother's body can dispose of them. The umbilical cord connects fetus to mother at the site of the future "belly button," or navel.

After several months, the fetus's body becomes pudgier and covered in a creamy substance, called vernix, that prevents the skin from becoming waterlogged.

uterus

placenta

umbilical cord

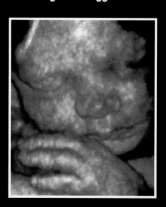

Most babies are born at around nine months and weigh between 6.5 and 7.5 pounds (3–3.5 kilograms).

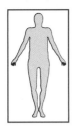

Increased medical knowledge regarding health, diet, illness, and treatments has lead to huge advances in the length and quality of our lives.

Children today average about an inch taller, for the same age, than children born one hundred years ago.

Two centuries ago, the average lifespan ranged from thirty to thirty-five years, even in the more-developed industrialized countries

👁 HEALTH WATCH

During the teenage years, small problems often seem gigantic—even when many teens share the same complaint. Overproduction of the natural skin oils of the face, neck, and back causes pimples (acne) and skin infections. Treatment includes careful hygiene and medicated ointments. Antibiotics help control bacterial growth that may worsen the condition.

Reproduction *Baby to Adult*

Most people do not reach complete physical maturity until about age twenty. Peak muscle power may occur a few years after that. But growing up is more than a physical process. "Mental maturity"—refining the attitudes, beliefs, and social skills of a unique personality—may take a lifetime.

Infancy and Childhood

From birth, a baby learns at an amazing rate. She learns the sounds, sights, and smells of her mother and family. After about six weeks, the baby learns that if she smiles, other people smile back and play with her, which makes life less boring than lying alone. At about five months, a typical baby sits up as her motor skills begin to develop further. Most babies crawl at eight months and take their first steps on about their first birthday.

A newborn baby can communicate with us. Instincts make her cry if something startles her, or when she feels hungry, too hot, too cold, or damp—like when her diaper needs changing.

At about age two, young children want to discover and explore. But they do not understand what danger means. This often leads to a battle of wills, which ends in the temper tantrums of the "terrible twos."

Child to Adult

At age two, most toddlers are about half their adult height, but their weight is only one-fifth of their expected adult weight. During childhood, growth gradually slows down. Then from about 9–12 years in girls, and a couple of years later in boys, growth speeds up again, and the body's shape and features change. During puberty, the reproductive system begins to function. Full sexual maturity takes up to four years for males and about two or three years for females.

Most teens spend less time with their families and more time with their peers (people their own age). Many new friendships become very intense very fast—then fade just as quickly.

🔊 GROWING UP FAST

Until puberty, girls and boys have similar body sizes and shapes. During puberty, the average male body grows taller and more angular, with broader shoulders, increased muscle volume, facial hair (*see left*), and a much deeper voice. The average female body also grows taller but becomes more rounded, with wider hips, developed breasts, and a slightly deeper voice than before.

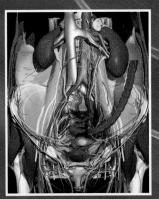

Glossary

abdomen the lower main body, from the base of the chest down to the hips.

alimentary canal the entire digestive tract, from the mouth to the anus.

appendix a fingerlike dead end in the lower right abdominal area that hangs from the large intestine, near the junction of the small intestine.

artery a strong, thick-walled blood vessel that usually carries blood away from the heart. Note: The two umbilical arteries from the fetus to the placenta convey oxygen-poor "blue" blood.

balanced diet moderately sized meals and liquids that contain a good mix of nutrients from all the food groups.

biodigester a type of septic tank that breaks down organic wastes (compost) and produces usable methane gas.

bladder a saclike body part that stores liquids, such as urine or bile.

capillary the tiniest vein or artery.

carbon dioxide a gaseous waste product produced during metabolism and breathed out through the lungs.

cartilage a strong, smooth, slightly flexible connective tissue that forms the nose, ears, and larynx and covers the ends of bones at the joints.

cells tiny building blocks of the body that form bones, muscles, skin, blood, and other organs and tissues.

chyme a slurry of liquified food that is ready for more complete digestion.

colon the large intestine.

dehydration lack of water.

dentin a tough living layer under the enamel coating of a tooth.

enamel the whitish or pale yellow covering of a tooth and the hardest substance in the body.

endocrine gland a gland that releases its juices directly into the bloodstream.

enzymes substances that help control the chemical processes in the body.

excretion removal.

gallbladder a small bag behind the liver that stores bile and passes it into the small intestine as needed.

gastric relating to the stomach.

goiter an abnormal enlargement of the thyroid gland caused by an iodine-deficient diet.

hepatic relating to the liver.

hormone a body chemical produced by an endocrine gland that circulates in the blood and controls a bodily function or change.

ligament a strong, straplike, slightly stretchy connective tissue that joins bone to bone and holds them together at the joints to allow for movement.

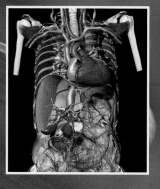

lymph a watery fluid that flushes the tissues of excess proteins and liquids and contains white blood cells and antibodies. It flows through its own set of vessels and filtering lymph nodes (lumps of lymph tissue) that parallel the circulatory system and empty into it.

metabolism the biological processes of life.

minerals inorganic substances, such as iron, calcium, iodine, sodium, or potassium, that the body needs in small amounts to remain healthy.

muscle a specialized tissue that contracts to make the body move.

nephrons tiny filtering units in the kidney that produce urine.

peristalsis moving waves of muscles along a tubelike body part.

puberty the time of life at which human sexual maturity begins.

renal related to the kidneys.

sphincter a round muscle.

umbilical cord the ropelike connection between the placenta and the fetus.

ureter a tube that drains urine from the kidney to the bladder.

urethra a tube that drains urine from the bladder to the outside world.

uterus (womb) the female reproductive organ where a baby grows and develops before birth.

vein a blood vessel with tiny internal valves that prevent the backflow of blood returning to the heart. Note: Not all veins carry dark, low-oxygen "blue" blood. The pulmonary veins (from the lungs to the heart) and the umbilical vein (from the placenta to the fetus) carry bright red, oxygen-rich blood.

vitamins chemicals found in food that the body needs in small amounts to stay healthy and work properly. Fresh fruits and vegetables contain many vitamins. Your body makes others, such as vitamins D and B_6.

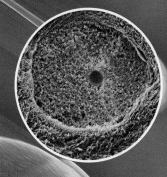

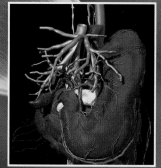

METRIC CONVERSION TABLE		
LENGTH		
1 inch = 2.54 centimeters		
SPEED		
1 foot per hour = 30 cm per hour		
WEIGHT		
1 pound (lb.) = 0.454 kilogram (kg)		
1 ounce (oz.) = 28.3 grams		
VOLUME		
1 cup = 0.236 liter		
ENERGY		
1 calorie = 4.184 joules		
1,000 joules = 1 kilojoule (kJ)		
1 calorie = 0.0042kJ		
9 calories/gram = 255 calories/oz.		
4 calories/gram = 113 calories/oz.		

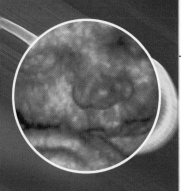

I n d e x

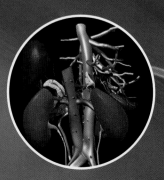